Ark...

Crom...id
by
John N. Merrill

Maps and photographs by John N. Merrill.

2001

My Derbyshire History Series.

Walk & Write Ltd.,
Unit 1, Molyneux Business Park,
Whitworth Road, Darley Dale,
Derbyshire, England. DE4 2HJ

Tel/Fax 01629 - 735911

email- marathonhiker@aol.com
WWW - members.aol.com:/marathonhiker

PUBLISHED BY - WALK & WRITE LTD.
TYPSET AND DESIGNED BY WALK & WRITE LTD.
PRINTED BY TRAIL PRESS.

© TEXT - JOHN N. MERRILL. 2000
© MAPS AND PHOTOGRAPHS - JOHN N. MERRILL 2000

ISBN 0-907496-35-0
FIRST PUBLISHED - 1986.
ENGLARGED AND UPDATED - NOVEMBER 2000

BRITISH LIBRARY CATALOGUING-IN-PUBLICATION DATA. A CATALOGUE RECORD OF THIS BOOK IS AVAILABLE FROM THE BRITISH LIBRARY.

TYPESET IN BOOKMAN BOLD, ITALIC, AND PLAIN 10PT, 14PT AND 18PT .

PLEASE NOTE - THE MAPS IN THIS GUIDE ARE PURELY ILLUSTRATIVE. YOU ARE ENCOURAGED TO USE THE APPROPRIATE 1:25,000 O.S. MAP.

JOHN MERRILL HAS WALKED ALL THE ROUTES IN THIS BOOK. METICULOUS RESEARCH HAS BEEN UNDERTAKEN TO ENSURE THAT THIS PUBLICATION IS HIGHLY ACCURATE AT THE TIME OF GOING TO PRESS. THE PUBLISHERS, HOWEVER, CANNOT BE HELD RESPONSIBLE FOR ALTERATIONS, ERRORS, OMISSIONS, OR FOR CHANGES IN DETAILS GIVEN. THEY WOULD WELCOME INFORMATION TO HELP KEEP THE BOOK UP TO DATE.

COVER DESIGN - BY JOHN N. MERRILL - WALK & WRITE LTD © 2000
COVER PHOTOGRAPH "MASSON MILL" - BY JOHN N. MERRILL © 2000

About John N. Merrill

Few people have walked the earth's crust more than John Merrill with more than 170000 miles in the last 30 years - the average person walks 75,000 miles in a lifetime. Apart from walking too much causing bones in his feet to snap, like metal fatigue, he has never suffered from any back, hip or knee problems. Like other walkers he has suffered from many blisters, his record is 23 on both feet! He wears out at least three pairs of boots a year and his major walking has cost over £125,000. This includes 89 pairs of boots costing more than £10,500 and over £1,500 on socks - a pair of socks last three weeks and are not washed.

His marathon walks in Britain include - -

Hebridean Journey....... 1,003 miles. Northern Isles Journey......913 miles.
Irish Island Journey ....1,578 miles.   Parkland Journey.......2,043 miles.
Land's End to John o' Groats.....1,608 miles.

and in 1978 he became the first person to walk the entire coastline of Britain - 6,824 miles in ten months.

In Europe he has walked across Austria - 712 miles - hiked the Tour of Mont Blanc, the Normandy coast, the Loire Valley (450 miles), a high level route across the Augverne(230 miles) and the River Seine (200 miles) in France, completed High Level Routes in the Dolomites and Italian Alps, and the GR20 route across Corsica in training! Climbed the Tatra Mountains ,the Transylvanian Alps in Romania, and in Germany walked in the Taunus, Rhine, the Black Forest (Clock Carriers Way) and King Ludwig Way (Bavaria). He has walked across Europe - 2,806 miles in 107 days - crossing seven countries, the Swiss and French Alps and the complete Pyrennean chain - the hardest and longest mountain walk in Europe, with more than 600,000 feet of ascent! He has walked 1,100 miles along the pilgrimage route from Le Puy (France) to Santiago (Spain) and onto Cape Finisterre. In the autumn of 2,000 he walked 270 miles from Prague to Vienna, across the Czech Republic.

In America he used The Appalachian Trail - 2,200 miles - as a training walk, before walking from Mexico to Canada via the Pacific Crest Trail in record time - 118 days for 2,700 miles. Recently he walked most of the Continental Divide Trail and much of New Mexico: his second home. He has walked the Chesopeake & Ohio Canal National Historical Trail and in 2000, 1,310 miles in Ohio, following The Buckeye Trail. In Canada he has walked the Rideau Trail - Kingston to Ottawa - 220 miles and The Bruce Trail - Tobermory to Niagara Falls - 460 miles.

In 1984 John set off from Virginia Beach on the Atlantic coast, and walked 4,226 miles without a rest day, across the width of America to Santa Cruz and San Francisco on the Pacific coast: His walk is unquestionably his greatest achievement, being, in modern history, the longest, hardest crossing of the U.S.A. in the shortest time - under six months (178 days). The direct distance is 2,800 miles.

Between major walks John is out training in his own area - The Peak District National Park. He has walked all of our National Trails many times - The Cleveland Way thirteen times and The Pennine Way four times in a year! He has been trekking in the Himalayas five times. He created more than thirty-five challenge walks which have been used to raise more than £600,000 for charity. From his own walks he has raised over £100,000. He is author of more than 180 walking guides which he prints and publishes himself, His book sales are in excess of 3 million, He has created many long distance walks including The Limey Way , The Peakland Way, Dark Peak Challenge walk, Rivers' Way, The Belvoir Witches Challenge Walk and the Forest of Bowland Challenge.

3

CONTENTS

Page No.

Introduction 5

Cromford Map...6

Arkwright of Cromford..7

Three Mile Walk...26

Cromford Mill - What to see today...................................32

Bibliographical Note..36

Other Books by John Merrill...38

My Derbyshire History Series 40

The Mill Manager's House, opposite Cromford Hill.

INTRODUCTION

Derbyshire has been home to many mechanical geniuses during the last three centuries - Sir Joseph Whitworth, renowned for Whitworth thread, lived in Darley Dale, near Matlock, for instance. Perhaps the most colourful figure of all was Sir Richard Arkwright, who by sheer hard work brought about a social, economic and mechanical revolution.

He has fascinated me for several years, and by walking around the Peak District you can see at first hand so many remains of 18th Century mill industries. Seeing these places I began to research into the Arkwright story, and slowly pieced together this book. It is not intended to be a scholarly masterpiece, but is an effort to portray what he achieved in the village of Cromford.

The first part of the book is his story. At the end you can follow a three-mile walk and see at first hand many of the sites associated with Sir Richard Arkwright, while exploring the Cromford Canal and High Peak Trail - more industrial archaeology remains. The Arkwright Society have extensively restored Cromford Mill - an on going project - and you can see at first hand part of his original mill complex.

Cromford is proud of its historical past and I hope this book makes your visit an informative one, to one of England's finest industrial archaeological areas.

Finally my thanks to The Arkwright Society for their help in checking the text and adding helpful comments and current known facts about Arkwright's life and the Cromford story.

Happy exploring!

John N. Merrill

BASIC ARKWRIGHT SITES IN CROMFORD

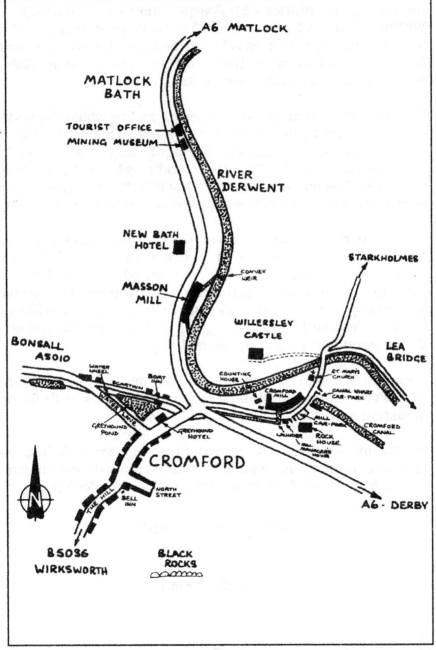

ARKWRIGHT OF CROMFORD.

Few men in the space of twenty four years have brought about such an abrupt and dramatic change in one industry. Between the years 1768 and 1792 Sir Richard Arkwright completely revolutionised the technical basis of the cotton industry transforming it from a cottage industry to an industry of world-wide proportions. Apart from developing machinery to do the work, he also created the factory system, which has earned him the title *"The Father of the Factory System'*, which is basically the same today. Arguably he may also be regarded as the first industrial tycoon in Britain. It is regrettable that for such an important and interesting person there are very few facts available about his mills or himself. Even his son, seven years after his father's death, found it extremely hard to gather accurate information.

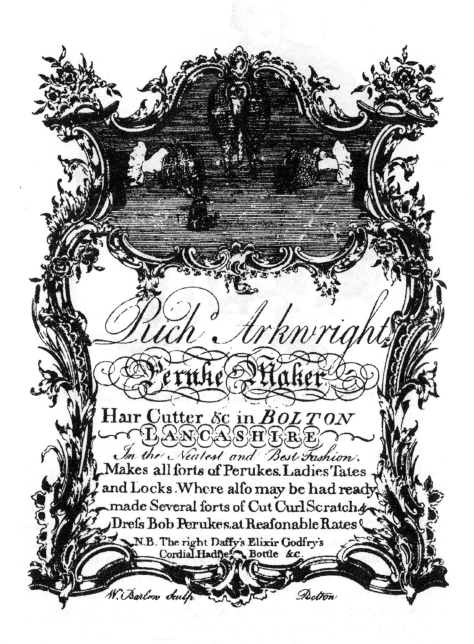

Richard Arkwright - Peruke Maker.

On 23 December 1732, Sir Richard Arkwright was born in Lord Street, Preston. He was the thirteenth child of a poor working family, and was named after his uncle Richard, who became his godfather. This was extremely fortunate, for his uncle was a learned man and took it upon himself to teach Richard how to read and write. Alas, Richard was not a very conscientious pupil, much preferring to be outside and playing with his friends. Later in his life he regretted not paying attention.

As soon as he was old enough, and much against his uncle's will, he was apprenticed to a barber named Nicholson in Kirkham, Preston, and became a 'lather boy'. At his uncle's insistence he continued to teach him - and Richard went to evening school during the winter months. At the age of eighteen, having successfully completed his apprenticeship, he moved to Bolton. There he was employed by Edward Pollit, a wig maker. By his drive and hard-working capacity Richard became Pollit's right-hand man, and was better at charming young ladies, who allowed him to buy their golden locks for making into wigs. Soon after his employment, his employer died, and Richard carried on the business for a time before starting his own in Churchgate, Bolton.

On 31 March 1755 he married his first wife, Patience Holt, in the parish Church. She was the daughter of Robert Holt, a schoolmaster of Bolton. This marriage was one of the few periods of his life when he was really happy. His business was flourishing, and although his barber's shop was below street level, it prospered. A sign outside said *"The Subterranean Barber - A Clean Shave for 1d"*. In the evenings he wrestled with a perplexing problem of finding a fast dye for his wigs. If it rained and the wig became wet, the dye simply ran out and stained the owner's coat. After hours of trial and error, he discovered a process, which he kept secret. He also played with mechanical devices, and in his shop he had a clock which, to the onlooker, appeared as though it was worked by smoke He was also in demand for bleeding people and pulling out painful teeth. This happy life abruptly ended, for his wife, Patience, gave birth to their only son on 19 December 1755. They called the boy Richard and were both deeply entranced by him; but after childbirth Patience grew weaker and eventually died.

For the next two years Richard continued working hard in his business, saving all the money he could. He was married again to Margaret Biggins of Pennington, on 24 March 1761. She had a small sum of money and with this she bought a better shop close to the White Bear public house. Business continued to expand, and he employed a journeyman to make strong country wigs, which were in fashion. Richard travelled the country, going to fairs and buying women's hair for his business.

On one of these travels in 1767 he met John Kay, a clockmaker from Warrington, which was a major turning point in his life. Working in Bolton and being in contact with so many people, he would have become familiar with the problems of spinning and weaving. Coupled with his natural ability in constructing mechanical contrivances, it is natural to suppose that he turned his attention to the problems of cotton spinning. There are several conflicting stories as to how he came to develop his spinning-machine, but it seems probable that this is the correct version. Arkwright showed Kay a mechanical device for perpetual motion. Kay like it, but told him there was a fortune to be made for the person who designed a spinning-machine.

Kay had worked for a person called Highs who tried to make such a machine, but it would not work properly and so he gave it up. However, he did try again later. Probably through this conversation, Arkwright learned sufficient about Highs' machine, and with his inventive brain he began working out a solution. First he asked Kay to 'bend him some wires and turn him some pieces of brass'. Working secretly, he next asked Kay to make him some models, so that he could perfect the solution. He became so engrossed in his task that he gave up his barber's business.

Having perfected the wooden models, Arkwright applied to Mr. Atherstone of Warrington, to make him a spinning-machine. Alas, because of Arkwright's shabby appearance, Atherstone declined, but offered to lend Kay a smith and a watch-tool maker to make the basic part of the machine. Kay undertook the clockmaker's part of it. There was a fear at this time that machines would deprive many people of jobs, and there was considerable resentment of anyone who tried to introduce them.

As a result, Arkwright and Kay went to Preston in January 1768, and with the financial backing of John Smalley, 'a liquor merchant and painter', began erecting the machine in the parlour of a house belonging to the Free Grammar School. Later, this building was converted into a public house, called the Arkwright Arms.

They went about their work in secret, but their movements aroused suspicion. a story was spread around that witchcraft was involved, as two women who lived close by heard *strange noises of a humming nature, as if the devil were tuning his bagpipes*. All the money Arkwright had went into the invention, for *'his clothes were in such ragged state that he declined, unless supplied with a new suit, to go to record his vote at the Preston Election of 1768.'*

With the new machine working properly he moved with Kay, in April 1768, to Nottingham, the centre of the hosiery industry. On 8 June 1769 he applied for a patent for the machine, and this was granted twelve months later, on 3 July 1769. Basically what Arkwright's machine did was to pass a strand of cotton through two sets of rollers. The first set of rollers compressed it, and its revolving motion passed it on to the next set of rollers. These were turning at a fast speed than the first set, thus lengthening the strand. From these rollers the cotton passed on to a revolving spindle which gave the twist to the yarn, before being wound round a bobbin. One of the advantages of the machine was that the spinner could spin several threads on the same machine, previously the work of several work people. The thread was also very strong, and ideal for warps because it was of a uniform thickness.

One of the key parts to the spinning-machine was the rollers. These were invented by Lewis Pail in 1738, but by this time the patent had expired. What Arkwright did in effect was ' poach' several ideas, and construct them into a spinning machine which was hardly altered in principle over succeeding generations. It was his inventive genius that accomplished this, but his driving force that brought the whole project to fruition.

In Nottingham he secured the financial support of two wealthy

Arkwright's original Spinning machine, 1769.
Photo - The Science Museum, London.

mill owners, Samuel Need and Jedediah Strutt. With their support he built a mill there, between Hockley and Woolpack Lane. For power to drive his machines he used horses, which proved far too expensive. However, the mill flourished, producing good yarn for the hosiery market. Because it was so successful he wanted to expand but found horse-power restricted this, and so he resolved to use another form of power. Water power was already being used successfully at Thomas Cotchett (better known as Lombe's and now an Industrial Museum) Silk Mill erected beside the Derwent in Derby in 1702.

Arkwright was frequently in the area, particularly in Wirksworth, and would have learnt that Cromford had a stream which never froze and a good supply of labour in the village and neighbourhood. Here he set up the first water powered cotton - spinning mill in the world. As a result his cotton- spinning machine came to be universally known as the 'water frame'. Today Cromford seems an odd place to build a mill, but in the eighteenth century it was ideal. It was close to Nottingham, the centre of the hosiery trade, and a road went through Cromford via Alfreton to Nottingham. It was centrally placed between Liverpool, Hull and London, the ports receiving raw cotton. Cotton arriving at Liverpool was carried to Derby by the Trent & Mersey Canal opened in 1778. From Derby it was brought by pack-horse to the Mill.

In 1771 Arkwright went into partnership with Samuel Need and Jedediah Strutt and he began erecting the first mill at Cromford, known as the Upper Mill. On 13 December 1771 Arkwright placed the company's first advertisement in the Derby Mercury advertising for clock makers, a smith, and offering employment to weavers and women and children. He was especially after large families. As the mill became more successful, he built homes for his workmen.

The best example of worker's housing is North Street in Cromford. The houses, built of gritstone, are three storeys high. The street is extremely wide, even by today's standards, and was built in 1777. Apart from the houses, Arkwright built a School, a Chapel and an Inn, known as the Greyhound. The Inn - the Greyhound Hotel still stands today, and the frontage

North Street, Cromford.

The Greyhound Inn, Cromford.

is practically unchanged. He also secured in 1790 the right to hold a Saturday market in the village, and fairs were to be held on 1st May and 1st October.

Cromford village today has been protected by a Conservation Order, as most of it still remains unaltered. It is possible to wander around and see at first hand the scene where industrial history was made. The original Mill still stands (see separate section) and the buildings are thirty feet wide, the width required to have two machines working opposite each other, with a central horizontal driving shaft. The Arkwright Society have opened the Mill to visitors and notice boards detail much of the history to be seen.

It is possible to walk from Cromford, following the road up the Via Gellia Valley for approximately one mile, then return following the water channels and five mill ponds. In the village it is possible to trace the water channels, which run underneath the A6 and into the original mill by means of a cast-iron launder. The launder proudly carries the date 1821, as it was fitted then, superseding the original wooden one erected in 1776. Here the building is only three storeys high. Originally it was five but the one upper storeys were removed following a fire in 1930.

Greyhound Pond, Cromford.

15

With the completion of the second Mill in 1776 Arkwright had
200 people working for him in the first Mill and 450 in the
second. When Masson Mill was built in 1784 he had over 800.
The males of the surrounding villages were all engaged in lead
mining, which meant that Arkwright had an abundant supply
of female and child labour. Wirksworth, two miles away, had a
population of well over 2,000, and villages like Bonsall and
Winster were close on 1,000.

Launder into the original mill - Cromford Mill.

Basically he worked the mills continuously, on two twelve-hour
shifts. Spinning was done at night, and carding during the
daytime. Again he set a precedent and set the following three
rules regarding the employment of child labour:

1. He did not employ children under the age of ten.
2. Expected to learn to read before entering the Mill.
3. Did not employ parish apprentices.

From the beginning he enforced scrupulous cleanliness and
systematic order. His workers worked a six-day week (72 hours)
so that Sunday was free for Church attendance.

The original part of Masson Mill.

John Byng, the fifth Viscount Torrington, wrote on visiting Cromford in 1790:

"The rural cot has given place to the lofty red mill and the grand houses of overseers; the stream perverted from its courses by sluices and aqueducts will no longer ripple and cascade. Every rural sound is sunk in the clamours of cotton works, and the simplest peasant is changed into the impudent mechanic".

He admitted that the Mills at night looked *'luminously beautiful.'*

William Bray on his tour into Derbyshire and Yorkshire in 1780, wrote: *"It employs about 200 persons, chiefly children, and to make the most of the term for which the patent was granted, they work by turns, night and day."*

Very few papers relating to Cromford Mill survive today and to give an example of Mill wages in the late 18th century, the following is taken from Arkwright's Bakewell Mill, managed by his son. The Wage Book, from 25 March 1786 to 10 May 1788. is quite informative about the conditions in the Mill. A breakdown of the week 25 March to 1 April 1786 shows that the Mill employed 480 people:-

286 Day Spinners	£51.6s.7d.	(£51.34p)
59 Night Spinners	£12.2s.2d.	(£12.11p)
38 Workmen	£18.9s.4d.	(£18.47p)
27 Cotton Pickers	£3.19s.81/2p.	(£3.98p)
48 Youlgreave Pickers	£6.11s.3d.	(£6.56p)
15 Youlgreave Rulers	£1.12s.1d.	(£1.61p)
12 Waste Pickers	£0.19s 0d.	(95p)
Total wage bill	£95. 0s.11/2d.	(£95. 01p).

Here is a sample extraction from the day-spinners' section of the Wages Book 25 March to 1 April 1786:

Day Spinners - 25 March - to 1 April 1786

No. Name	No4	d	h	s	d		s	d	
137 Howard, Thos.	4		6	3	9	(18p)	3.9	(18p)	
138 Howard, Am.	2		6	2	9	(14p)	2.9	(14p)	
139 Ingleby,Thos.	4		6	5	3	(26p)	5.3	(26p)	
140 Ingleby, In.	4		6	4	9	(24p)	4.9	(24p)	

Column 4 was divided into six columns which, I assume, represent working days of the week. In some cases an 'A' was marked, meaning absent, or a figure representing hours worked on the given day.

Arkwright was a very understanding employer, and was exceedingly fair and by no means a tyrant. He even paid overtime, for there are entries such as - 'S Wheldon - 3 hours overtime - 41/2d (2p)' There is one entry for the period 15-22 April 1786: Wm. Woodward, 10 days ill at home from an accident, allowed ...5/3d (26p)' Intermingled with the wages are entries for piecework on spindles and rollers, for example:

'9th September to 16th 1786 - Spencer, Thos. 15 dozen spindles turned ... 17/6d (88p).' 18th November to 25th, 1786 - 42 dozen rollers ... 5/3d (26p).'

18

It was largely because of his fairness towards his workers that he was able to expand his industry to mammoth proportions. John Byng, on his visit in 1790 found a eulogy pinned to the Greyhound Inn door. It was written by an old women and ran as follows:

"Come let us all here join in one,
And thank him for all favours done;
Lets thank him for all favours still
Which he hath done besides the mill.
Modestly drink liquor about,
And see whose health you can find out;
This will I chose before the rest
Sir Richard Arkwright is the best.
A few more words I have to say,
Success to Cromford's market day."

He lent money to employers so that they could buy a cow, and *' he gave distinguishing dresses to the most deserving workers and arranged balls at the Greyhound Inn, where he could show them off.'*

In September 1776 he inaugurated his annual festival of 'candle-lighting,' which became for his workers the highlight of the year. Some 500 workers and children led by a band and with a young boy working a weaver's loom, would march round the Mill and village. On returning to the mill, everyone was given buns, nuts, fruit and ale. In the evening there was music and dancing.

In 1776-77 he built another Mill at Cromford, known as the Lower Mill. During the next seven years Arkwright built several more mills in the Derbyshire area, namely Cressbrook in 1779, Rocester, Near Uttoxeter, 1781; Ashbourne 1781; Bakewell 1782; Wirksworth 1783; and Masson Mill in 1784. They were all driven by water and worked on lines which he had perfected at his original Mill in Cromford. By 1787 there were 22 Mills in Derbyshire and this figure rose to 37 in 1803. Masson Mill is still operative, and was sold to the English Sewing Cotton Co. in 1897. The Mill has been extensively enlarged but one can easily identify the original building. High on its frontage a plaque records *'Sir Richard Arkwright & Co. 1769-1969, 200 years*

service to the industry.' If the visitor looks over the wall he can
see the weir and diversion in the River Derwent so that the
water could be brought into the Mill to drive the machinery.
The weir is unusual, being convex and not concave in shape.

Meanwhile with his perfection of the spinning-machine,
Arkwright began expanding his interests and inventing other
machines. To achieve this

*'Arkwright commonly laboured in his multifatious concerns from
five o'clock in the morning 'till nine at night; and when
considerably more than fifty years of age, feeling that the defects
of his education placed him under great difficulty and
inconvenience in conducting his correspondence and in the general
management of his business, he encroached upon his sleep in
order to gain an hour each day to learn English grammar and
another to improve his writing and orthography (correct spelling)'*

In 1773, Arkwright began turn his attention to the manufacture
of calico. Instead of using a linen warp, as previously, he used
a thread warp, and in conjunction with a cotton weft he produced
a cloth which was made solely from cotton for the first time in
England. Although it met with a great demand, the Calico Act
of 1736 demanded a double duty. This was a prohibitive figure,
which made the manufacture almost uneconomical. On 25
February 1774 a petition against this was presented to the House
of Commons by the Arkwright company. On 1 June 1774
changes in the law were passed by the Lords and given Royal
Assent, fourteen days later. The excise duty was fixed at 3d
(2p) per yard. All British cotton stuffs had to have three blue
strands in the selvage to identify it against foreign calico. This
gave a tremendous boost to the home industry. In 1775 the
total manufacture of British calico was 56,814 yards, whereas
2,111,439 yards were imported. Eight years later the picture
was completely reversed, with only 770,922 yards imported and
a total of 3,578,590 yards of British manufacture.

On 16 December 1775 Arkwright took out a patent covering ten
machines, including a carding machine known as a 'roving'
machine. Previous to this, strands of cotton had to be joined
together by hand before they could be spun. By using a metal

comb worked by a crank, he brought the cotton out of the carding machine in a continuous length. He also employed rollers, which, by running at different speeds, made the cotton strand stronger and more uniform in thickness.

During his life he suffered many setbacks. In 1777 he started a Mill at Birkacre, near Chorley, his first Mill outside Derbyshire, two years later in 1779, when the Lancashire workers were having a recession in their trade, they attacked several Mills, smashing the machines of both Arkwright's and Hargreaves' spinning-jennies. Bickacre was attacked and was completely destroyed, and Arkwright never rebuilt the Mill. Several people were prosecuted and jailed, including a woman, for twelve months. Arkwright, during these troublesome times, kept Cromford ready to meet the rioters. They never came to within fifty miles of Cromford. It was probably just as well, for they would have met with a large welcoming party. Within an hour, Arkwright could assemble over 600 men, 1,000 guns and several cannons.

On 14 April 1781, Samuel Need died. With him went the partnership. No records remain of the financial settlement. Arkwright kept his Cromford Mills, and Strutt retained the Mills at Belper and Milford. Six months after Need's death, the Nottingham Mill was destroyed by fire. Arkwright rebuilt this, and it remained in the Arkwright family until 1809.

Despite these setbacks his industry continued to advance quickly in 1784 he went to Glasgow, where he was treated like royalty being given a dinner, made an Honorary Burgess and a Guild Member. After the dinner he was shown the Clyde valley and the falls of the Clyde. With this volume of water he could easily drive his machinery and in 1785 David Dale's New Lanark Mills were being built and were operative in 1786.

Because of Arkwright's dominant position in the cotton-spinning industry, he was not liked by the Lancashire manufacturers, quite understandably, when one realises that the cotton industry was growing at an unprecedented rate. Between the years 1776 and 1781, the net import of raw cotton was about 6 million pounds a year. From 1782 to 1784 it was double this figure, and the following three years it was treble that amount. The one place where Arkwright was vulnerable was his patents. This specification, which was in the name Richard Arkwright, of Nottingham, Clockmaker, was scant and misleading and was often being disputed, The whole issue came to a head, and a trial took place in London in June 1785. The jury had to decide on three points:

1. Is the invention new?
2. Was it invented by the Defendant?
3. Was it sufficiently described in the specifications?

As there was not conclusive evidence to satisfy all three points, the verdict went against Arkwright. This made his machine available to all, but because of his production schemes, he retained his leading position.

Having achieved commercial success and become the richest commoner in the land, he let his son become more and more involved in the running of the mills. His son completely looked after Bakewell Mill, which had a turnover of at least £20,000 per year. Having in the space of twenty-five years, built up a personal fortune of £500,000, Arkwright began seeking social success. On 22 December 1786, he gave a congratulatory address to King George III, from the Wapentake of Wirksworth after his escape from assassination by Margaret Nicholson. Afterwards Arkwright was knighted but it was not merely for his speech but as recognition for his work in the cotton industry.

The following year, 1787, Arkwright was appointed High Sheriff of Derbyshire. He went into his year's office with the same drive and thoroughness that he used in his Mill. Wherever he went, the scene was exceedingly lavish, as Arkwright had richly attired his coachmen and had a glittering carriage. Although he was extremely rich, he was equally generous not only to his family but to his friends and workers often giving his children large sums for Christmas. By contrast his workers had to card, pin and reel 5,040 yards of cotton per day for only 4d. Although this amount is small, his workers were better off than most at this time.

Up to this time, 1788, Arkwright had lived in a large house opposite his Cromford Mills, known as Rock House. The only thing he lacked was a mansion. As a result he purchased a large estate from William Edward Nightingale, the father of Florence Nightingale, for £20,000. Close to the Mills and overlooking the Derwent, he planned to build his castle.

Willersley Castle and the River Derwent.

He employed William Thomas, an architect from London. Before Willersley Castle, as it is called, could be built, a large boulder had to be excavated and its removal cost Arkwright £ 3,000. When the building was almost complete, a fire badly damaged the castle on 8 August 1791. It was rebuilt, but was not completed until after Arkwright's death. The castle is now a conference centre, and is set among delightful woodlands, since he had planted 100,000 trees.

For many years Arkwright had suffered from asthma, but despite this he had worked amazingly hard and created the impossible. Steam engines were being tried at his Nottingham Mill, and a canal from his Cromford Mill was being excavated. 'He would make light of discussions on taxation and say that he would pay the National Debt.' However, on 3 August 1792 he died, aged sixty.

To end this brief biography on this remarkable man of the Industrial Revolution, Stephen Glover wrote in his "Peak Guide", published in 1830, that on coming to Matlock:

"The road was now impassable from the crowds of people who had assembled to witness the procession of Sir Richard Arkwright's funeral on its way to Matlock Church.

Ceremony was conducted with much pomp, and as nearly as I can remember was thus - a coach and four with the clergy; another with the pall-bearers; the hearse, covered with escutcheons, surrounded by mules, followed then the horse of the deceased, led by a servant; the relations and about fifteen to twenty carriages closed the procession, which was nearly half a mile in length."

A fitting end would be hard to find. He was buried at Matlock Church, but his remains were later moved to St. Mary's Church, Cromford, when it was completed in 1797. originally intended as a private Chapel for Willersley Castle; many of the Arkwright family were buried here.

St. Mary's Church, Cromford.

CROMFORD WALK - 3 MILES

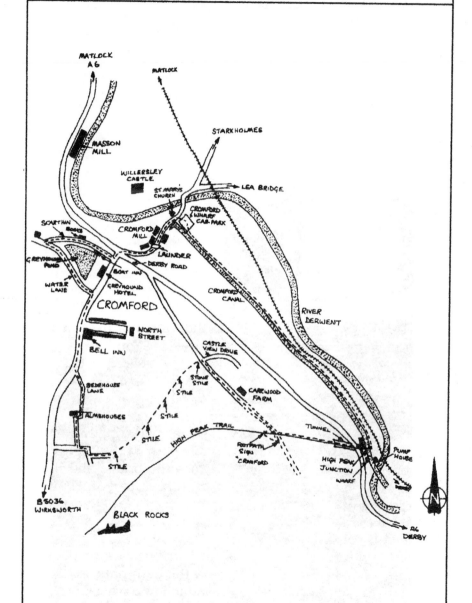

CROMFORD - 3 Miles
- Allow 2 hours.

Map O.S. 1:25,000 Outdoor Leisure Series - The White Peak - East Sheet.

Car Park: Cromford Wharf.

Early Closing Day - Thursday.

Inns - The Greyhound Inn and Boat Inn, Cromford.

Teas - Cromford and Masson Mill.

ABOUT THE WALK- In 1771 Richard Arkwright started a cotton spinning Mill here which led to a huge industry in Derbyshire and the Midlands. He developed the factory system and is today known as *'The Father of the Factory System.'* On this walk you see at first hand many of his original buildings - Mills and workers houses - while walking beside a canal ascending a unique railway line, now a pedestrian way. You pass several Inns, can visit Arkwright's original Cromford Mill complex, and visit the Arkwright Heritage Museum in Masson Mill - the remainder of the building is now a tasteful shopping village.

WALKING INSTRUCTIONS- From the car park walk up to the canal and turn left, and follow the tow path to the High Peak Junction, just over a mile away. Cross the bridge and begin ascending the High Peak Trail, passing through a tunnel under the A6 road. Before crossing the canal you can extend the walk a short distance to see the wharf and Pump House. Ascend the trail for a third of a mile, and shortly after passing a small building on your right you reach a path sign on your left - 'Cromford'. Leave the trail and follow the path past, and walk through the tunnel under the trail and follow a walled path for the next 1/2 mile.

Pass Carrwood Farm on your right and enter a housing estate. Just before Castle View Drive on your right, leave the road and follow the distinct stiled path on your left for just over 1/4 mile. Keep straight ahead on the road and follow it to your right then left. Turn right down Bedehouse Lane, which becomes a tarmaced path in the middle. At the bottom turn right and descend the main road - 'Cromford Hill' - to central Cromford. On the way you pass North Street on your right.

At the bottom of the hill turn left along Water Lane, and 300 yards later turn right along 'Scarthin' and pass Scathin's Bookshop and the Boat Inn. Turn left at the end to the A6 road. Cross over to the right and descend the road past the original Arkwright Mill to the start of the Cromford Canal and car park. You can extend the walk, by 1/2 mile, to your left along the A6 road to visit Masson Mill.

HISTORICAL NOTES - in walking order.

CROMFORD CANAL - Although it was opened after his death in 1793, Sir Richard Arkwright had been greatly involved with the Canal. The Canal was 14 1/2 miles long, and joined the Erewash Canal at Langley Mill, it cost £80,000 to build. The Canal enjoyed many years of use until the coming of the railway to Matlock in the 1860's. By 1900 it was closed to through traffic because of the collapse of the Butterley Tunnel.

The start of the Cromford Canal.

LEAWOOD PUMP HOUSE - To maintain the water level in the canal, this pump House was built in 1840 to pump water from the River Derwent. Inside is the original Graham & Co. beam engine. When operating it can lift between 5 and 6 tons of water a minute. Nearby is the aqueduct over the River Derwent. Open on specific days during the summer months.

HIGH PEAK JUNCTION - To link the Cromford Canal with the Peak Forest Canal at Whaley Bridge a canal was proposed. but, because of the hilly terrain of the Peak District, it was not practical. Instead, a railway with nine inclines was built and operating in 1831. The 33-mile journey took two days, and up each incline the wagons had to be hauled. It was never a viable railway, and the last section closed in 1967. Since then, a 17-mile section from here to Dowlow, near Buxton, has been converted to a pedestrian way. The incline you ascend is known as the Cromford Incline and is 580 yards long and a 1 in 9 gradient. A museum and Information Centre at the start of the incline gives fuller information. Toilets and icecream available.

NORTH STREET - Cromford is now a conservation area, and much of the housing dates from the late 18th Century, being build by Sir Richard Arkwright for his workers. These three-storeyed buildings are amongst the finest examples of industrial archaeology to be found in England.

MILL POND - To feed water to Arkwright's original Mill, a series of five mill ponds were constructed-this is the last one. From here the water passes through tunnels and a channel before crossing the road in a cast-iron lauder (dated 1821) into the Mill.

GREYHOUND HOTEL - Built by Sir Richard Arkwright in 1788. The splendid Georgian front has remained unaltered since then. Close by is the Boat Inn built in 1772.

MASSON MILL - Just along the A6 road and built by Arkwright in 1783 was operating for more than 200 years. The building has been converted to a shopping complex and a Heritage Museum details Arkwright's life and cotton spinning. The weir is unusual, being convex instead of the normal concave.

WILLERSLEY CASTLE - Sir Richard Arkwright lived in Rock House on the right of the Mill, but in 1788 began building his Castle. Before work could commence, a large boulder was removed at a cost of £3,000. By 1791 the building was almost complete when a fire badly damaged it. Arkwright died the following year and never took up residence.

CROMFORD MILL- Arkwright's original Mill, built in 1771. The Mill operated almost continuously, with whole families working a twelve-hour shift. The Mill is open to the public - see separate section.

CROMFORD MILL SITE
- WITH BUILDING DATES

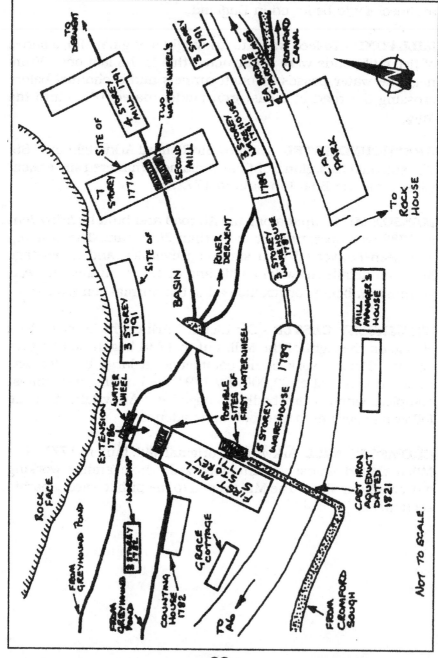

Not to scale.

CROMFORD MILL - What to see.

Cotton spinning ceased in the mid 19th century here. Mills were no longer dependent on water power, operating by steam power, so the industry moved from Derbyshire to Lancashire, although Masson Mill still operates today. The Cromford site was used for other purposes, but fire in 1890 destroyed the second Mill, although its outline can still be traced. Other parts served as a brewery, a laundry and more recently a colour works. In 1979 the Arkwright Society acquired the site. The task before them is an on going one, demolishing some of the other buildings not associated with Arkwright's Mill, restoring buildings, creating a museum, and excavating the site. A visit gives a fascinating insight into what Arkwright achieved.

For me the enjoyment of the site is to be able to see at first hand where history was made. The original Mill still stands and the clear straight mortar line of its extension can be seen. The launder enters the site to where possibly the second waterwheel was located on the side of the building. The first was possible at the building's northern end - where the extension is, with another wheel on the end of that. The water courses can be seen with the basin where the water could be regulated to the second Mill, to the Cromford Canal or to the River Derwent. Excavations are revealing the courtyard floor, the site of a smelting works before Arkwright's occupancy and foundations of the second Mill. On your visit take time to wander around and absorb the scene, walk along the road and see the launder, Mill Manager's House, the Cromford Canal and St. Mary's Church.

Historic photograph of my neighbour working on a machine in Masson Mill in the mid 1980's.

Masson Mill today - now a shopping village in the historic mill with the entrance on the left to the working museum.

Bibliographical Note.

The following books and articles contain data relating to Arkwright:-

F. Andrews (ed) the TORRINGTON DIARIES (1954 ed).

Anon, THE MATLOCKS (official Guidebook. 1970).

M. Arkwright. COTTON ARKWRIGHT - biographical word (1971).

W. Bray. SKETCH OF A TOUR INTO DERBYSHIRE AND YORKSHIRE (1783 ed).

S.D. Chapman. THE EARLY FACTORY MASTERS (Newton Abbot, 1967).

C.Charlton. P.Strange and D. Hool. ARKWRIGHT AND THE MILLS AT CROMFORD (Arkwright Society).

R.S. Fitton and A.P. Wadsworth. THE STRUTTS AND THE ARKWRIGHTS (Manchester, 1958).

Stephen Glover. THE PEAK GUIDE (1830).

R. Guest. A COMPENDIOUS HISTORY OF THE COTTON MANUFACTURE WITH A DISPROVAL OF THE CLAIM OF SIR RICHARD ARKWRIGHT TO THE INVENTION OF THE INGENIOUS MACHINERY (Manchester (1823).

F.C. Mutton. DERBYSHIRE (1939).

F. Nixon. THE INDUSTRIAL ARCHAEOLOGY OF DERBYSHIRE (Newton Abbott, 1969).

James Pilkington. A VIEW OF THE PRESENT STATE OF DERBYSHIRE 2 vols.(1789).

J.B. Robinson. DERBYSHIRE GATHERINGS (1866).

J. Tann. 'Richard Arkwright and Technology', History (February 1973) 29-44.

B. Taylor. RICHARD ARKWRIGHT - THE MAN OF THE MILLS (1957).

Victoria County History. DERBYSHIRE. Vol.11.

A.P Wadsworth and J. Mann. THE COTTON TRADE AND INDUSTRIAL LANCASHIRE (Manchester. 1931).

Water basin in Cromford Mill complex.

OTHER JOHN MERRILL WALK BOOKS

CIRCULAR WALK GUIDES -
SHORT CIRCULAR WALKS IN THE PEAK DISTRICT - Vol. 1,2 and 3
CIRCULAR WALKS IN WESTERN PEAKLAND
SHORT CIRCULAR WALKS IN THE STAFFORDSHIRE MOORLANDS
SHORT CIRCULAR WALKS - TOWNS & VILLAGES OF THE PEAK DISTRICT
SHORT CIRCULAR WALKS AROUND MATLOCK
SHORT CIRCULAR WALKS IN "PEAK PRACTICE COUNTRY."
SHORT CIRCULAR WALKS IN THE DUKERIES
SHORT CIRCULAR WALKS IN SOUTH YORKSHIRE
SHORT CIRCULAR WALKS IN SOUTH DERBYSHIRE
SHORT CIRCULAR WALKS AROUND BUXTON
SHORT CIRCULAR WALKS AROUND WIRKSWORTH
SHORT CIRCULAR WALKS IN THE HOPE VALLEY
40 SHORT CIRCULAR WALKS IN THE PEAK DISTRICT
CIRCULAR WALKS ON KINDER & BLEAKLOW
SHORT CIRCULAR WALKS IN SOUTH NOTTINGHAMSHIRE
SHIRT CIRCULAR WALKS IN CHESHIRE
SHORT CIRCULAR WALKS IN WEST YORKSHIRE
WHITE PEAK DISTRICT AIRCRAFT WRECKS
CIRCULAR WALKS IN THE DERBYSHIRE DALES
SHORT CIRCULAR WALKS FROM BAKEWELL
SHORT CIRCULAR WALKS IN LATHKILL DALE
CIRCULAR WALKS IN THE WHITE PEAK
SHORT CIRCULAR WALKS IN EAST DEVON
SHORT CIRCULAR WALKS AROUND HARROGATE
SHORT CIRCULAR WALKS IN CHARNWOOD FOREST
SHORT CIRCULAR WALKS AROUND CHESTERFIELD
SHORT CIRCULAR WALKS IN THE YORKS DALES - Vol 1 - Southern area.
SHORT CIRCULAR WALKS IN THE AMBER VALLEY (Derbyshire)
SHORT CIRCULAR WALKS IN THE LAKE DISTRICT
SHORT CIRCULAR WALKS IN THE NORTH YORKSHIRE MOORS
SHORT CIRCULAR WALKS IN EAST STAFFORDSHIRE
DRIVING TO WALK - 16 Short Circular walks south of London by Dr. Simon Archer Vol 1 and 2
LONG CIRCULAR WALKS IN THE PEAK DISTRICT - Vol.1,2 3, and 4
DARK PEAK AIRCRAFT WRECK WALKS
LONG CIRCULAR WALKS IN THE STAFFORDSHIRE MOORLANDS
LONG CIRCULAR WALKS IN CHESHIRE
WALKING THE TISSINGTON TRAIL
WALKING THE HIGH PEAK TRAIL
WALKING THE MONSAL TRAIL & OTHER DERBYSHIRE TRAILS
40 WALKS WITH THE SHERWOOD FORESTER by Doug Harvey
PEAK DISTRICT WALKING - TEN "TEN MILER'S" - Vol 1 & 2
CLIMB THE PEAKS OF THE PEAK DISTRICT
PEAK DISTRICT WALK A MONTH Vol One and Vol Two
TRAIN TO WALK - Vol 1 - THE HOPE VALLEY LINE

CANAL WALKS -
VOL 1 - DERBYSHIRE & NOTTINGHAMSHIRE
VOL 2 - CHESHIRE & STAFFORDSHIRE
VOL 3 - STAFFORDSHIRE
VOL 4 - THE CHESHIRE RING
VOL 5 - LINCOLNSHIRE & NOTTINGHAMSHIRE
VOL 6 - SOUTH YORKSHIRE
VOL 7 - WALKING THE TRENT & MERSEY CANAL
VOL 8 - WALKING THE DERBY CANAL RING
VOL 9 - WALKING THE LLANGOLLEN CANAL

JOHN MERRILL DAY CHALLENGE WALKS -
WHITE PEAK CHALLENGE WALK
DARK PEAK CHALLENGE WALK
PEAK DISTRICT END TO END WALKS
STAFFORDSHIRE MOORLANDS CHALLENGE WALK
THE LITTLE JOHN CHALLENGE WALK

NORTH YORKSHIRE MOORS CHALLENGE WALK
LAKELAND CHALLENGE WALK
THE RUTLAND WATER CHALLENGE WALK
MALVERN HILLS CHALLENGE WALK
THE SALTER'S WAY
THE SNOWDON CHALLENGE
CHARNWOOD FOREST CHALLENGE WALK
THREE COUNTIES CHALLENGE WALK (Peak District).
CAL-DER-WENT WALK by Geoffrey Carr,
THE QUANTOCK WAY
BELVOIR WITCHES CHALLENGE WALK
THE CARNEDDAU CHALLENGE WALK
THE SWEET PEA CHALLENGE WALK

INSTRUCTION & RECORD -
HIKE TO BE FIT.....STROLLING WITH JOHN
THE JOHN MERRILL WALK RECORD BOOK
HIKE THE WORLD

MULTIPLE DAY WALKS -
THE RIVERS'S WAY
PEAK DISTRICT: HIGH LEVEL ROUTE
PEAK DISTRICT MARATHONS
THE LIMEY WAY
THE PEAKLAND WAY
COMPO'S WAY by Alan Hiley

COAST WALKS & NATIONAL TRAILS -
ISLE OF WIGHT COAST PATH
PEMBROKESHIRE COAST PATH
THE CLEVELAND WAY
WALKING ANGELSEY'S COASTLINE.

MY DERBYSHIRE HISTORICAL GUIDES -
A to Z GUIDE OF THE PEAK DISTRICT
DERBYSHIRE INNS - an A to Z guide
HALLS AND CASTLES OF THE PEAK DISTRICT & DERBYSHIRE
TOURING THE PEAK DISTRICT & DERBYSHIRE BY CAR
DERBYSHIRE FOLKLORE
PUNISHMENT IN DERBYSHIRE
CUSTOMS OF THE PEAK DISTRICT & DERBYSHIRE
WINSTER - a souvenir guide
ARKWRIGHT OF CROMFORD
LEGENDS OF DERBYSHIRE
DERBYSHIRE FACTS & RECORDS
TALES FROM THE MINES by Geoffrey Carr
PEAK DISTRICT PLACE NAMES by Martin Spray

JOHN MERRILL'S MAJOR WALKS -
TURN RIGHT AT LAND'S END
WITH MUSTARD ON MY BACK
TURN RIGHT AT DEATH VALLEY
EMERALD COAST WALK
JOHN MERRILL'S 1999 WALKER'S DIARY
A WALK IN OHIO - 1,310 miles around the Buckeye Trail

SKETCH BOOKS -
SKETCHES OF THE PEAK DISTRICT

COLOUR BOOK:-
THE PEAK DISTRICT.......something to remember her by.

OVERSEAS GUIDES -
HIKING IN NEW MEXICO - Vol I - The Sandia and Manzano Mountains.
Vol 2 - Hiking "Billy the Kid" Country. Vol 4 - N.W. area - " Hiking Indian Country."
"WALKING IN DRACULA COUNTRY" - Romania.

VISITOR GUIDES - MATLOCK . BAKEWELL. ASHBOURNE.

John Merrill's
"My Derbyshire"
Historical Series

A TO Z GUIDE TO THE PEAK DISTRICT by John N. Merrill .... 0 907496 89 X....£3.50

WINSTER - A SOUVENIR GUIDE. by John N. Merrill.............. 0907496 81 4.................£2.50.

DERBYSHIRE INNS - AN A TO Z GUIDE. by John N. Merrill........ 0907496 71 7.............£4.50.

HALLS & CASTLES OF THE PEAK DISTRICT. by John N. Merrill....0907496 72 5......£3.95.

ARKWRIGHT OF CROMFORD by John N. Merrill.............. 0 907496 35 0.............£4.50.

DERBYSHIRE FACTS AND RECORDS by John N. Merrill .... 1 874754 12 8...........£3.00

PEAK DISTRICT PLACE NAMES by Martin Spray ...... 0 907496 82 2....................£3.25

THE STORY OF THE EYAM PLAGUE by C.Daniel ......ISBN 0 9523444 0 8..£6.95

THE EYAM DISCOVERY TRAIL & 1858 RAMBLE by Clarence Daniel ....£3.50.

PEAK DISTRICT SKETCH BOOK - ....ISBN 1 874754 02 0................................£5.00

GHOSTS & LEGENDS -

DERBYSHIRE FOLKLORE. by John N. Merrill...........0 907496 31 8.......................£5.95.

DERBYSHIRE PUNISHMENT by John N. Merrill.................... 0 907496 33 4.............£3.00.

CUSTOMS OF THE PEAK DISTRICT & DERBYS by J. N. Merrill .... 0 907496 34 2.....£3.50

LEGENDS OF DERBYSHIRE. by John N. Merrill.............. 1 874754 00 4....................£3.95

NEW TITLES IN PREPARATION -

LOST INDUSTRIES OF DERBYSHIRE by John N. Merrill £6.95

DERBYSHIRE HISTORY THROUGH THE AGES -

Vol 3 - DERBYSHIRE IN NORMAN TIMES by John N. Merrill £4.50

Vol 1 - DERBYSHIRE IN PREHISTORIC TIMES by John N. Merrill £4.50

CHURCHES OF DERBYSHIRE by John N. Merrill £4.95

DERBYSHIRE IN MONASTIC TIMES by John N. Merrill £4.50